Getting Started

Materials You Will Need

water	eyedropper	pennies
glass	plastic soda bottle	paper
card	cork	jar & lid
pan	stick	flashlight
fork	slide projector	bucket
spoon	ice cube	rope
toothpick	paper towel	straws
salt	tin cans	cloth

Opening Activity

A good way to launch into this series of activities is to draw attention to the fact that learning is a lifelong process that lasts long after you are out of school and long after you are away from home. When there are no parents or teachers to answer questions, how do you figure things out for yourself?

How do you figure out what the problem is when:

- the car stops running?
- the dog gets sick?
- your friend gets mad at you?
- you've lost an instruction manual?

Get the ball rolling by playing "Twenty Questions" with your class. Then show how you can adapt that game to a questioning strategy solving scientific mysteries. Explain how "yes-no" questioning can be used in situations where no one is able to answer. A doctor can ask a patient, "Does this hurt?" A veterinarian can't ask a dog, but can push the spot and see if the dog yelps. A mechanic can't ask a car if it is leaking oil, but he can test for the answer by putting paper under the car and looking for oil spots later.

Teaching Students the Inquiry Process

Instructions for the Teacher

After playing "Twenty Questions" as an opening activity, teach this more refined version of the inquiry process using the scientific mysteries in this book. Start with the example described on the poster to explain the process to your students. Then apply the process to the other mysteries.

Explain how the "inquiry" process works:

- Students observe a demonstration of a scientific mystery.
- Students observe carefully and make simple notes on copies of the form on page 4.
- Students ask "yes - no" questions of the teacher or other designated demonstrator to find an explanation.
- Each questioner keeps the floor until he/she yields.
- Other students listen to all questions and answers.
- If discussion is needed, halt the questioning and provide a "conference period" with a time limit.
- When the questioning starts again, there should be no more conferencing.
- If the students bog down, provide hints, but make the participants get the explanation out of you with questions.
- Discuss the final answer and confirm your students' understanding of that scientific principle. Have them write it on their form.
- Discuss how they found their way to the explanation. Highlight the value of both "yes" and "no" answers in finding explanations.
- Discuss the significance of the scientific principle they have discovered. Have them make notes about the significance on their form.
- Help students to apply the inquiry process to everyday problems they run into.

Note: You can also prep students to be the demonstrator and to answer the questions.

The Mysteries

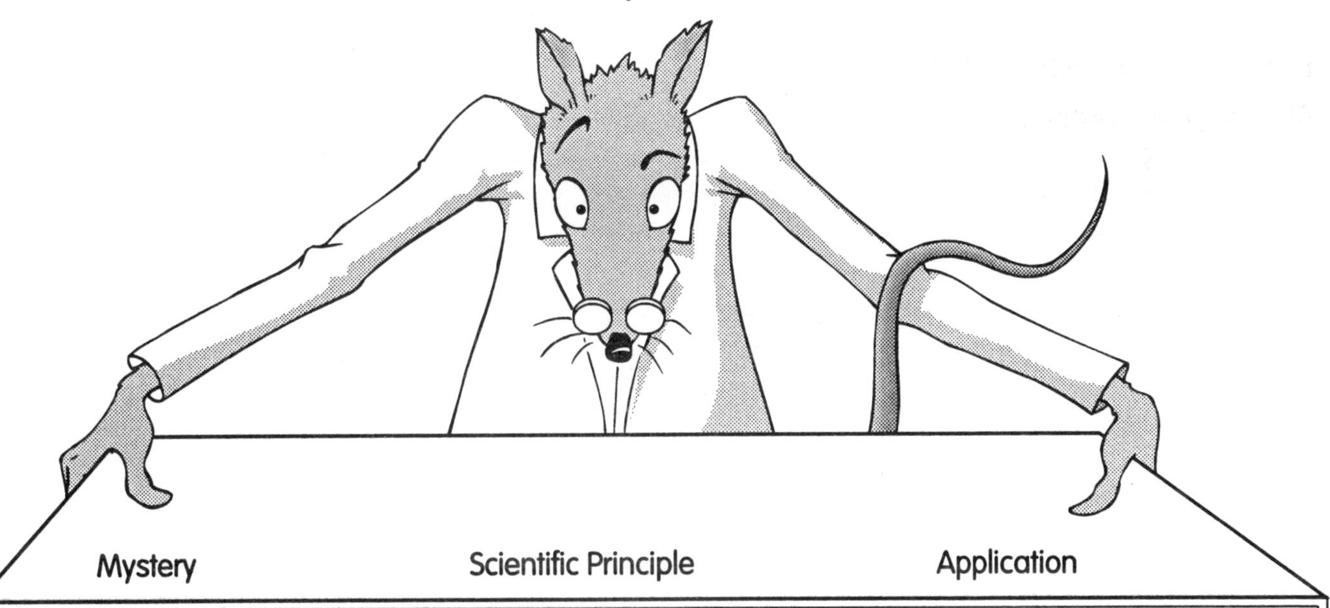

Mystery	Scientific Principle	Application
1. Lifting Water	*Atmospheric Pressure*	Pumps making water go uphill
2. Over the Edge	*Center of Gravity*	Cranes that don't topple over
3. 1 + 1 = 1?	*Solubility*	Drinkable medications
4. Sink or Float	*Buoyancy*	Ships, submarines
5. A picture in Thin Air	*Persistence of Vision*	Movies, Television
6. It's Only the Tip	*Crystalization*	Keeps lakes from freezing solid
7. Water Running Uphill	*Adhesion, Capillarity*	Plant circulation, paper towel use
8. Head for the Border	*Cohesion, Surface Tension*	Rain falls as drops
9. Goofy Wheels	*Inertia, Center of Gravity*	Balancing car wheels
10. Well, Blow Me Down!	*Bernoulli Principle, Lift*	Causes airplanes and birds to fly
11. Pouring Light	*Internal Reflection*	Fiber Optics

Name ______________________

Date ______________________

Title for this science mystery:

____

What's going on here?

Make sketches and write notes that show and tell what you observe before you start thinking about the explanation for what you are seeing. Develop questions you could ask to find out what is happening.

What is causing this?

____

____

____

____

____

____

What is this principle called? ______________________

How is knowledge of this principle used?

____

____

____

____

____

____

Lifting Water

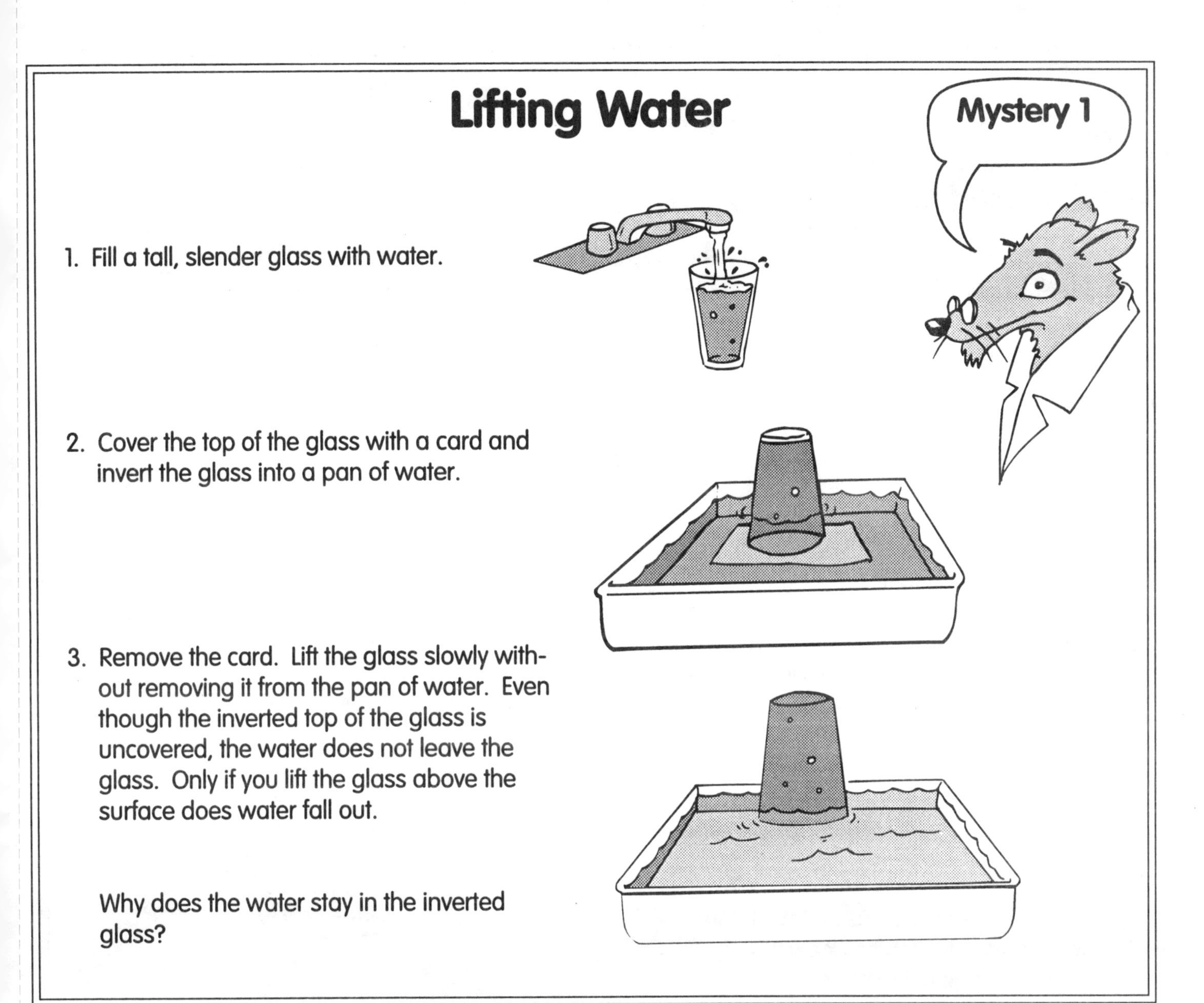

1. Fill a tall, slender glass with water.
2. Cover the top of the glass with a card and invert the glass into a pan of water.
3. Remove the card. Lift the glass slowly without removing it from the pan of water. Even though the inverted top of the glass is uncovered, the water does not leave the glass. Only if you lift the glass above the surface does water fall out.

Why does the water stay in the inverted glass?

The explanation:

The atmosphere is like an ocean of air. The farther down an object is in that body of air, the more pressure there is. The pressure is caused by the weight of the air above. The pressure of air on the surface of the water in the pan is greater than the weight of the water in the glass. That air pressure pushes the water up into the glass. When the glass is raised above the surface, air can get up into the glass. Then the air pressure pushing down is as great as the air pressure pushing up. The weight of the water (gravity) makes the water fall.

The significance:

Air pressure at sea level pushes harder than the weight of a column of water over 30 feet (over 10 meters) high. As a result, we can use air pressure to pump water up into water towers. Then, when we open our faucets, gravity pushes it back down from the tower through pipes with an even flow.

The Scientific Principle

<u>Atmospheric pressure</u> pushes in all directions.

Over the Edge

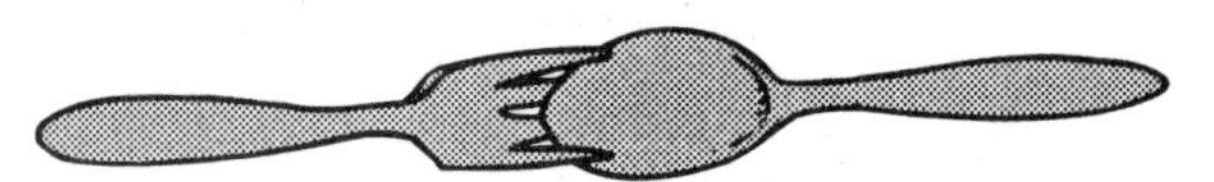

1. Hook a fork and a spoon together by wedging the big end of the spoon between the tines of the fork.

2. Put one end of a toothpick between the center tines and the other end on the edge of a glass of water. Believe it or not, if you move the fork, spoon and toothpick back and forth slowly, they will come to a point where they balance by themselves.

3. The teacher can even use a match to burn off the part of the toothpick extending inside the edge of the glass.

   If the silverware and remaining toothpick are completely outside the glass, why don't they fall?

The explanation:

Although it appears that this is out of balance, the way the spoon and fork curve around the glass makes the collective center of their weight at the point where the toothpick meets the glass.

The significance:

Giant cranes can lift heavy weights without tipping because an equal amount of weight is on each side of the crane. Swim racers can lean out over the water at the start without falling if they hold their arms out behind them to balance their head and put their center of gravity over their feet.

The scientific principle:

Objects balance at their center of gravity.

1 + 1 = 1?

1. Fill a glass as full of water as you can - so full that if you added one more drop of water, it would spill over.

2. Now add salt a little at a time, allowing each portion to dissolve before adding the next amount.

   Why are you able to add so much salt without the water overflowing?

The explanation:

When a solid is dissolved in a liquid, the solid molecules are able to move around and fit between the molecules of the liquid without pushing them apart. Only after the in-between space is all taken up will any additional salt sink to the bottom and overflow the water.

The significance:

Many solid materials are sold in liquid form because they will be easier or more appealing to use that way. It is easier to distribute a material evenly if it is dissolved in a liquid. The active ingredients in many liquid cosmetics and medicines are actually solids dissolved in a non-medicinal liquid..

The scientific principle:

Solubility - solids can be dissolved by liquids and become evenly distributed within them.

Sink or Float

1. Pull enough water into an eye dropper so that it will *barely* float in a glass of water.

2. Remove the label from a family-size plastic soda bottle. Fill the bottle with water almost to the top.

3. Move the eyedropper from the glass to the bottle without losing any water. Put the cap on the bottle.

4. Squeeze and release the bottle to make the eyedropper go up, down, or hover. Do this gently so that the students can't tell what you are doing.

   What is making the eyedropper move up and down?

The explanation:

Objects sink until they displace their own weight of water. When you squeeze the bottle, it forces water into the eyedropper. That makes it heavier, so it sinks. When you release the pressure, the air in the eyedropper expands and pushes some of the water out. Now it is lighter, so it floats up.

The significance:

Ship builders don't spend millions to build boats just in the hope that they will float. They figure out exactly how much the ship will weigh, including people and cargo. Then they figure out how far down the ship will have to sink to displace that weight of water.

The scientific principle:

Bouyancy - a floating body sinks low enough to displace its own weight of water.

A Picture in Thin Air

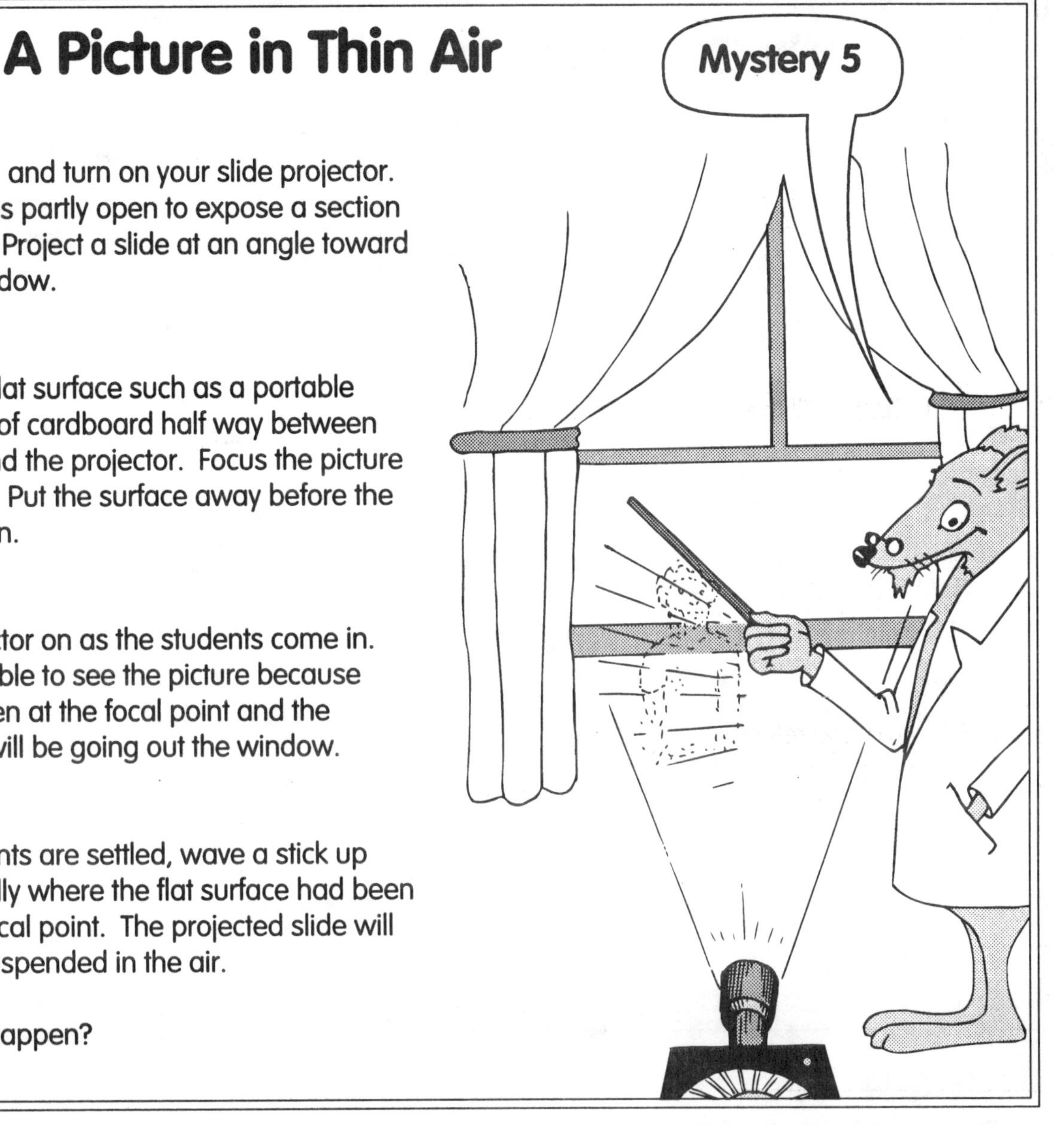

1. Darken the room and turn on your slide projector. Leave the curtains partly open to expose a section of the windows. Project a slide at an angle toward the exposed window.

2. Now hold up a flat surface such as a portable screen or piece of cardboard half way between the windows and the projector. Focus the picture on that surface. Put the surface away before the students come in.

3. Leave the projector on as the students come in. They won't be able to see the picture because there is no screen at the focal point and the projected light will be going out the window.

4. When the students are settled, wave a stick up and down rapidly where the flat surface had been placed at the focal point. The projected slide will appear to be suspended in the air.

   Why does this happen?

The explanation:

The stick sends parts of the picture to your eye, piece by piece. Your eye continues to see each part until the next part is visible. Your brain blends the parts into a continuous impression.

The significance:

Without persistence of vision, you wouldn't be able to look at a moving picture. Movies are made of separate still shots shown in quick succesion. It is up to your eyes and brain to blend them into a smoothly changing image.

The scientific principle:

Persistence of vision - your eye sends images to your brain for a little longer than they are actually visible.

The explanation:

Water molecules rearrange themselves into crystals when they freeze. That is unusual. Because the crystal formation keeps the molecules apart, the volume of the ice is one-eleventh more than the water it came from. Therefore, ice floats with one-eleventh of itself above the water level.

The significance:

Now we know why ships run into icebergs. The icebergs are almost entirely under water, but they still float. Even more significant is the fact that if ice didn't float, seas and lakes would freeze from the bottom up. That would make them completely solid, instead of having a protective sheet of ice on top with liquid water below. That would wipe out the plant and animal life that lives in them.

The scientific principle:

Crystallization can increase the volume of a solid.

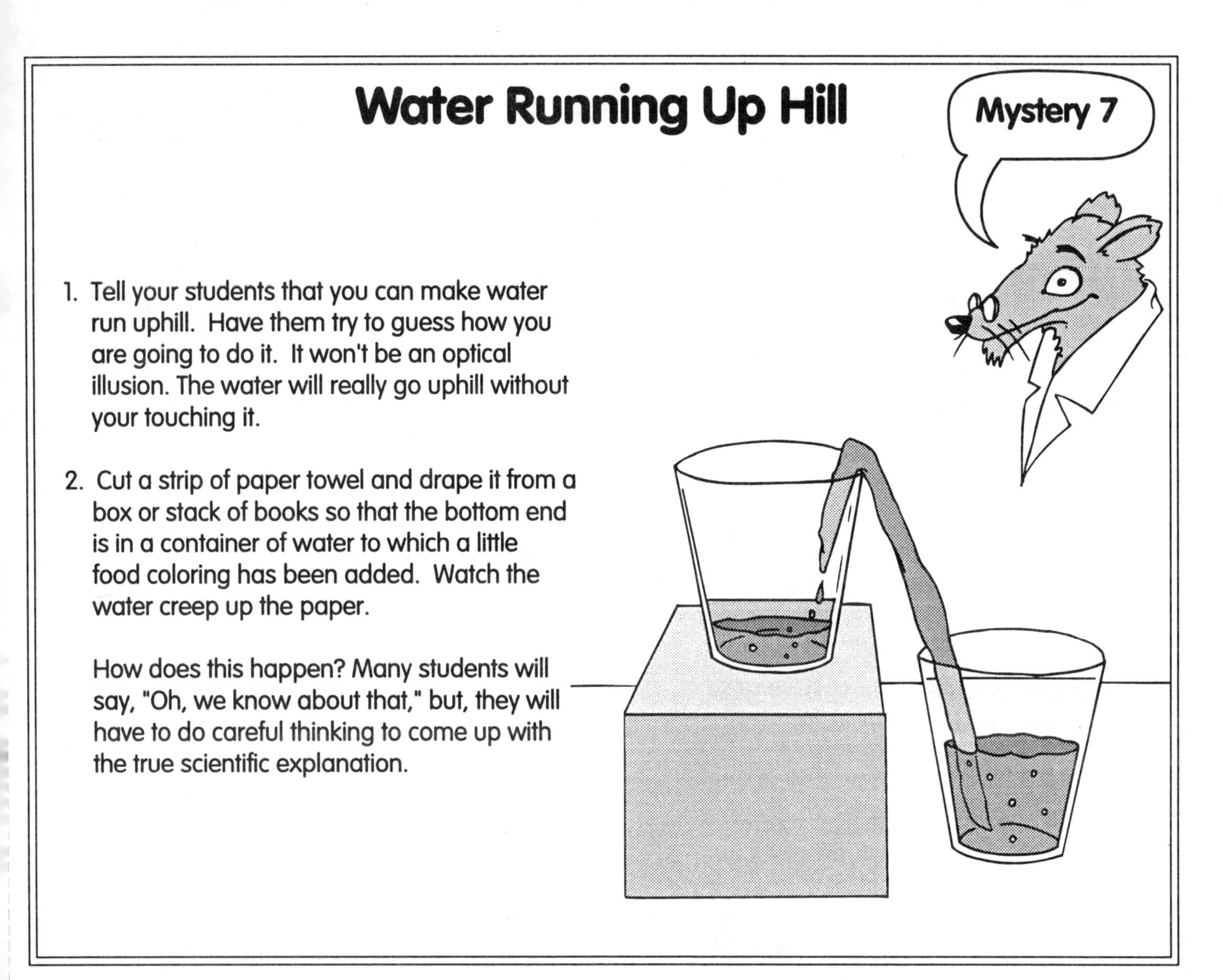

Water Running Up Hill

1. Tell your students that you can make water run uphill. Have them try to guess how you are going to do it. It won't be an optical illusion. The water will really go uphill without your touching it.

2. Cut a strip of paper towel and drape it from a box or stack of books so that the bottom end is in a container of water to which a little food coloring has been added. Watch the water creep up the paper.

   How does this happen? Many students will say, "Oh, we know about that," but, they will have to do careful thinking to come up with the true scientific explanation.

The explanation:

As the water molecules wiggle, they spread out. Molecules of two different types tend to stick to each other. As the water molecules spread, they climb up and cling to the fibers in the paper, filling the spaces between the fibers. The smaller the spaces, the easier for the molecules to climb and fill them in.

The significance:

Capillarity is how water gets from the roots of plants up into their stems and leaves. Without capillarity, paper towels wouldn't work.

The scientific principles:

<u>Molecular Motion</u> - all molecules "wiggle."
<u>Adhesion</u> - unlike materials cling together.
<u>Capillarity</u> - liquids climb into small spaces.

Head for the Border

1. Fill a glass close to overflowing with water.

2. Put a cork into the glass of water. Push the cork to the center of the glass.

3. Observe what happens to the cork.

   Why does the cork keep floating over to the edge, no matter how many times you push it to the center?

The explanation:

Make sure to fill the glass as full as you can. In fact, have the students look at the water after the activity to see that it is well above the rim of the glass without spilling over. Water has sort of a "skin" on its surface. When you fill the glass above the rim, the skin makes a dome shape with a high spot in the middle and sloping in all directions toward the edge. The cork is merely drifting downhill toward the edge.

The significance:

If there were no cohesion or surface tension, there would be no clouds or raindrops. Rivers and seas would evaporate. Water would be evenly distributed around the world, partly in the air and partly clinging to solid objects.

The scientific principles:

Cohesion - molecules of liquid cling together.

Surface Tension - cohesion at the surface of a liquid forms a skin-like cover.

Goofy Wheels

1. Before students come to class, remove both ends of three identical cans. Replace them with reclosure lids. If you can see through these lids, paint them or cover them with tape.

2. Secretly tape an equal number of pennies inside each can, positioning them differently each time:

   Can #1: all stacked together across the middle
   Can #2: evenly distributed around the edge
   Can #3: all stacked up at one place at the edge

3. As the students watch, roll the three cans down an incline. Some roll smoothly. Some roll with a jerky motion. Some roll faster than others. What is making the difference?

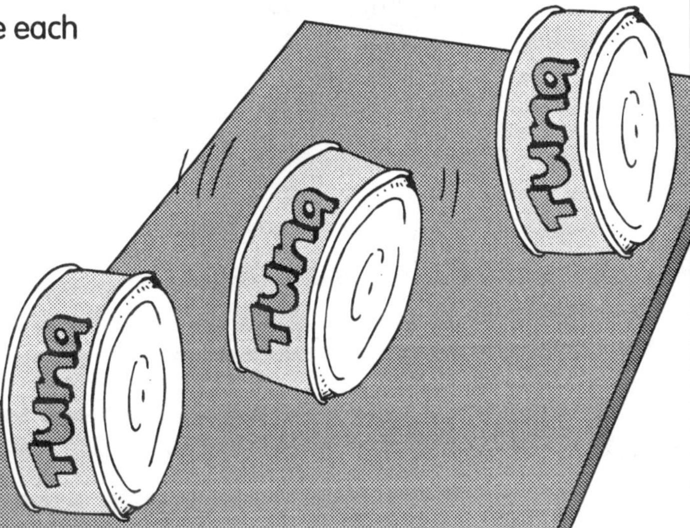

The explanation:

#1 will roll fast and smoothly because the weight is evenly distributed and centrally placed.

#2 will roll more slowly at first but smoothly. The weight is evenly distributed, but it takes more force to move the can with the weight at the edge.

#3 will move with a jerky motion because the weight is off center, moving the center of gravity away from the middle of the can.

The significance:

Mechanics have to "balance" car wheels by putting weights on the rim to make up for imperfections in the shape of the tire. Without those counter-balances, the car will feel "jerky" when the wheels turn.

The scientific principles:

Inertia - It takes more force to move weights at the edge because the weights have to move further for the can to turn.

The center of gravity must be in the middle of a wheel for it to roll smoothly.

Well, Blow Me Down!

1. Hold a piece of paper by two adjacent corners so that the near edge is level, but the far edge hangs down.

2. Blow across the **top** of the paper. Observe what happens to the paper.

   Why does the paper lift up toward the moving air instead of down away from the stream of air?

The explanation:

Moving air exerts less pressure than air that is not moving. When you blow across the top of the paper, the moving air exerts less pressure on the top of the paper than the still air below it. The greater pressure below pushes the paper up.

The significance:

This is what makes birds and airplanes fly. The bottom surface of a wing is flat, but the top surface has a bulge. Air passing over the top has to move faster to go around the bulge. Since it is going faster than the air below the wing, it doesn't push down as hard as the slower air below is pushing up. The resulting upward push is called "lift."

The scientific principle:

Moving air exerts less pressure than still air.
(This is referred to as the Bernoulli principle.)

Pouring Light

Mystery 11

1. Before students come in, tape a flash light to the bottom end of a slender jar.
2. Poke two holes in the opposite edges of the jar's lid using a hammer and nail.
3. Roll dark construction paper around the flashlight and jar, and tape it in place.
4. Fill the jar about 2/3 full with water. Put the lid back on the jar. Turn on the flashlight.
5. Tell your students that you can pour light just like pouring water.
6. Darken the room and "pour light " through the bottom hole in the lid into a container.

What is happening here?

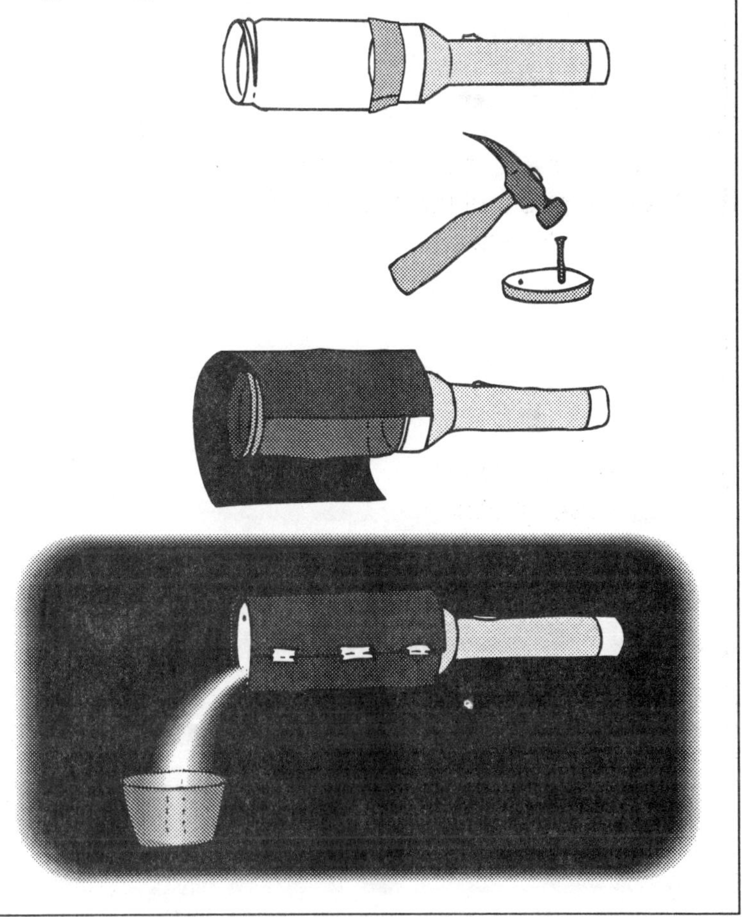

The explanation:

When you pour the water through the lower hole, the light will be trapped within the flowing water because it bounces back from the water's surface when it hits the surface at a shallow angle.

The significance:

Optical fibers made of fiberglass are replacing electric wires for carrying telephone and computer messages. The signals are carried by light that is trapped by internal reflection and carried along inside the tiny fibres of glass.

The scientific principle:

When you look into the front of a fish aquarium and try to see someone standing at the side of the aquarium, you can't see through the side. When light gets inside the glass, it gets trapped in there. It bounces off the inside surfaces of the glass unless it hits the glass straight on. Instead of seeing the person standing to the side of the aquarium, you see images reflected from inside. This trapping of light is called internal reflection .

Note: Use everyday materials from around your school or home and the poster included in this unit to explore other science mysteries and their significance.

More Mysteries to Solve

Mystery	Scientific Principle	Significance
Defying Gravity  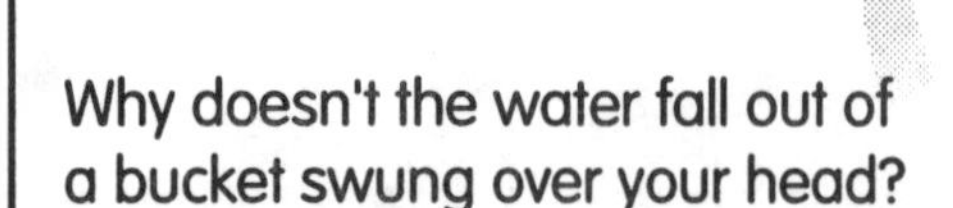 Why doesn't the water fall out of a bucket swung over your head?	**Momentum** is the tendency to keep going in the same direction you are moving.	Momentum forces you into your seat as you do the loop on a thrill ride.
Tablecloth Pull  Why do objects stay on the table when you quickly pull a slippery tablecloth away?	**Inertia** is the tendency of an object at rest to stay put. **Friction** is the rubbing together of rough surfaces.	Oil and grease are used to make objects slippery when you want them to move without friction.
Where's the Penny?  Why can't you see a penny under a glass of water if you put a card on top of the glass? (You are looking from the side.)	**Refraction** bends light, but not enough to come out the side of the glass. The card blocks your view where the image of the penny does come out.	Glasses, microscopes and telescopes all bend light by refraction to focus the rays. This makes objects look clearer or larger.
Rolling Ice Cube  Why does an ice cube roll over and over in warm water?	**Stability** occurs when most of the weight is below the center of gravity, When ice melts at the bottom, there is more weight on top so the ice rolls.	They build ships that don't roll over by putting balast (weight) at the bottom of the ship.